REGISTERED

By Michelle J. Miller

Self-Published

www.michellejmillerlaw.com

Printed in the United States of America

ISBN 978-1-7346862-2-7

Special discounts are available on bulk quantity purchases by book clubs, associations, organizations, special interest groups, conference hosts and workshop facilitators. The author is also available for speaking engagements, coaching and training on the contents of this book as well as other topics. For details email: info@michellejmillerlaw.com or call (312) 985-5200.

CONTENTS

DEDICATION

I dedicate this book d to the doers! I dedicate this book to innovators, trailblazers, pioneers, creative geniuses, and dreamers, who decided to make a difference. I also dedicate this book to my clients, who trust me to develop strategies to protect their brands, businesses, and bucks.

I especially dedicate this book to Dr. Lynn Richardson and MC Lyte. Lynn and Lyte. Lynn and Lyte, thank you for allowing me to share my wisdom, knowledge, and experience on trademarks (and other intellectual property issues) at "The W.E.A.L.T.H Experience" because the experience changed my life; it pushed me into purpose. Lynn and Lyte, this book results from your faithful creation of a W.E.A.L.T.Hy place for women to be productive and prosperous in every area of life.

Michelle J. Miller

INTRODUCTION

"Live your best life by handling & protecting your business."
- Michelle J. Miller-Boston

L et's get right down to business. If you have dreamed of starting a business, if you have a side gig, or if you are a business owner, this book is for you! Creating and maintaining a business can be overwhelming, but you conquer challenges when handling your business. There are no shortcuts to success; you must put in the work. Successful people make sacrifices that unsuccessful people refuse to make. Successful people know protecting their brands create a strong business foundation.

I wrote this book was to help guide people like you through the challenge of protecting their brands with registered trademarks. Protecting your brand is an essential tool for protecting your business and your bucks. As an attorney with over 20 years of legal and business experience, I wrote this book to help you handle your business. I wrote this book to help you protect your intangible business assets, your intellectual property – particularly your trademarks. I am privilege to work with celebrities, entertainers, ministry leaders, authors, influencers, coaches, literary agents, publishers, entrepreneurs, business owners, and executives on business and brand issues. I have spent many years providing legal advice on marketing, e-commerce, business, and regulatory compliance issues to business leaders on a local, national, and international level in the corporate world. Then I opened my law practice to help my clients navigate brand and business issues in the global marketplace. This guide will be your go-to resource, and I promise you will review it again and again.

I want you to make informed decisions about your business(es) and your brand(s). Securing trademarks for your brand(s) is a cost-effective way to reduce business risks and increase business value. This book is a guide designed to give you practical knowledge about protecting your brand. This book will help you understand the trademark registration process. This book is not a substitute for seeking legal advice; the content is not legal advice. I hope it encourages you to seek the services of an experienced attorney.

This guide will help you gain an understanding of intellectual property with a focus on trademarks. My motivation for writing this book is simple: I'm passionate about assisting people in owning and growing their businesses and protecting their brands. I hope this guide will encourage you to protect your brand before infringement occurs. My career as an attorney includes handling business issues on a local, national, and international level, including reviewing and negotiating multi-million-dollar contracts. I have witnessed smart people make not-so-smart decisions that have had a detrimental impact on their businesses, brands, and bucks. You will be the smart person that makes wise business decisions. You will not have to learn the hard way from this day forward. This book will guide you through a necessary process, the process of obtaining a registered trademark to protect your brand. It is time for you to get your brands REGISTERED!

1

MIND YOUR BUSINESS

—————————— ⌒⌒∞⌒ ——————————

*"Mind your business and stop worrying about your non-existent competition.
Your competition does not exist because no one does what you do like you do it!"*
- Michelle J. Miller-Boston

Mind your business. This chapter is titled "Mind Your Business" because that is what you need to do to handle your business. I remember adults saying "mind your business" as a kid, and I would get upset. However, as an adult, I soon recognized that minding my business is the best thing to handle my business. Today, I am happy to mind my business. I want you to be satisfied with minding your business. You are about to live and breathe your dreams. Whether you are sitting at your job thinking about jumping into entrepreneurship or an experienced business owner, this chapter will ignite you to protect your business. This book is for doers, ones that will dream big and then take significant actions. If you are a dreamer only, this book is not for you. This book was written as a guide to help people wake up from their dreams and do the work to take their lives and their businesses to the next level. So, let's get down to business.

DEFINE YOUR WHY

I want to start this journey by igniting you to take proactive steps to protect your brand, business, and bucks. To do that, I need to light a fire of passion within you, and I believe this comes through you recognizing your purpose – your why. I need you to identify the foundation of why you do what you do. Let's start by defining your WHY.

List the reasons why you do what you do. If you want to start something new (i.e., a business, ministry, etc.), why do you want to create it? Write your reason below.

_____

_____

_____

One of your "whys" should be that you are passionate about what you are doing or what you plan to do. When you are passionate about something, you invest your time and money in it. If you lack passion, you lack purpose, and without these two things, you will not value what you do enough to protect it. If you are passionate about sharing your gifts and talents with the world, you will recognize the value in what you do. If you realize the value of what you do, you can define success for yourself.

IDENTIFY YOUR NICHE

I started this chapter with a quote that I often tell myself. To sum it up, the quote reminds me that I am special. The quote reminds me that no matter how many people do what I do, they can never do it as I do it. Your niche is your specialty and your unique way of delivering that specialty to the world. I hate to break this to you, but you cannot be a specialist in 50 different things. You can have various income streams, but you cannot be a specialist in everything you touch.

Your unique style determines the types of projects you take on and the type of customers and clients you attract. News flash: you can't be everything to everyone, so please stop trying. Set your standards, operate in excellence, and stand by your business position. Many people know me as a Christian business and brand lawyer who loves to travel and interact with people of all different ethnicities, races, genders, religious beliefs, and backgrounds. I have a reputation for operating in integrity and honesty. My ideal clients are wise goal-getters who are not afraid to take risks and who love to laugh, handle business, and enjoy the finer things in life. In other words, they are a lot like me, or they need someone like me in their lives to push them to their next level.

In the next section, define your niche. Identify what makes you unique and identify why people would want to work with you.

_____

_____

_____

_____

_____

CREATE YOUR DEFINITION OF SUCCESS

I did not ask you to write the dictionary's definition of success in this section. To the contrary, I am asking you to "CREATE YOUR DEFINITION OF SUCCESS" because there is a difference. One of the beautiful things about building your own business and brand is that you get to define what success looks like to you.

To one-person success looks like owning a global multimillion-dollar brand, but to another person, success looks like providing business ownership opportunities to single moms. When you define success for yourself, you determine what success looks like to you.

The pathway to success is not a straight road; it is a journey full of twists and turns that you're willing to go on because it is worth every step. The individuals you are connected to, or your social media followers, determine what success looks like in your life.

In this section, write your definition of success.

_____

_____

_____

_____

_____

_____

_____

_____

_____

_____

After you "DEFINE YOUR WHY," "DEFINE YOUR NICHE," and "CREATE YOUR DEFINITION OF SUCCESS," it is crucial to identify any perceived obstacles that you need to overcome. You must identify these obstacles to develop a plan of attack. Every day it can feel as if there are a million obstacles that stand in your way of success. However, you are an overcomer. You can overcome any obstacle that comes your way. How do I know? Because if you're reading this book, you are unstoppable. No matter what hits you, you are like that Energizer® Bunny; no matter what happens, you refuse to give up or give in, you are still going! You might be your obstacle. For example, you may think you are not smart enough, educated enough, or you're not talented enough, but you must overcome these thoughts. Whatever obstacles you face, you can overcome them because you can get up and do something about them. Put in the work, position yourself as an expert, and then do this one simple thing – act like you are who you say that you are.

Identify your obstacles below and whether they are real or imaginary. Proclaim the following daily: "*I am an overcomer, and I will overcome every obstacle that comes my way!*"

OBSTACLE	REAL	IMAGINARY
_____	☐	☐
_____	☐	☐
_____	☐	☐
_____	☐	☐
_____	☐	☐
_____	☐	☐

Now that you have identified your perceived obstacles and whether they are real or imagined, it is time for you to develop a plan of attack. You cannot just identify obstacles and let them stay there. After you identify obstacles that stand in your way of success, you must develop a plan to deal with them. If you do not create a plan to deal with your obstacles, you will always experience defeat, which is true even if all of your blocks are imaginary. Imaginary obstacles remind me of what I've heard people say about the word "FEAR" – they say fear is FALSE EVIDENCE APPEARING REAL. Sometimes obstacles appear real, but they are figments of our imagination because we have not been through the experience yet. Your attack plan may require that you develop a strategy to overcome the perceived obstacles you have created in your mind. Use the section below to write a brief plan of attack to overcome obstacles.

YOUR PLAN TO ATTACK YOUR OBSTACLES

_____

_____

_____

_____

ENCOURAGE YOURSELF

You must mind your business to ensure that you take time to encourage yourself as you handle your business. Starting and growing a business can be discouraging as you walk along your journey towards success. As you walk along your journey, you must learn how to become your own greatest fan. Before we dig deeper into protecting your business, brands, and bucks with trademarks, I want you to recognize that the most important thing you must protect is your peace of mind. You will get frustrated sometimes, and you may feel scared and may even make some mistakes, but it's ok. You got this. Now, in the space below, write some words of encouragement to yourself.

_____

_____

_____

_____

_____

_____

_____

_____

2

BUILDING A PROTECTABLE BRAND

─────────── ⚬⟲⟳⚬ ───────────

"You are your brand! Wearing brands is not the goal; being a brand is."
– Michelle J. Miller-Boston

B uild a protectable brand. Many people think about logos, graphics, and color combinations when they hear the word "branding." However, creating a protectable brand requires more than pretty colors and your overall brand identity. Building a protectable brand involves research and a personal determination to be unique instead of copying others. A protectable brand is a brand that will pass the legal tests for federal trademark registration with the United States Patent and Trademark Office ('USPTO"). A protectable brand is a unique and robust brand. When determining your business name and your brand's other components, it is important to develop a strong and unique brand before spending your bucks!

PERSONAL BRANDING

You are your brand. Let's start by doing an overview of personal branding because this has significantly merged with business branding in the global marketplace. Personal branding is the practice of marketing yourself with your career or business. Personal branding has expanded from the corner office to Wall Street's hallways to Hollywood's red carpets to the viral video clips on social media.

Building a strong personal brand identity is integral to building a strong business brand. Close your eyes and envision what you want people to see when they think about you. Can you imagine yourself building great business relationships, collaboration opportunities, and loyal clients with the person you envisioned? Building a strong personal and business brand is an integral part of bringing the image you just saw in your head to life. Branding is more than just pretty graphics; it is the experience someone has with you and your business.

Your core values as a person, and business owner impact how people view your business. Core values are your fundamental personal, organizational, and business values that guide your behavior, and they are the unique pathway for achieving your business goal. For example, integrity, ethics, and honesty are my core values. When I think about my personal and business branding position, I envision people identifying me as a trusted advisor with a high moral standard with a vested interest in their success.

In the section below, write a personal brand vision, and as you write it, remember to make sure this vision reflects your core values:

_____

_____

_____

_____

_____

_____

I provide legal services to ministry leaders, entertainers, singers, actors, producers, speakers, coaches, and other highly paid professionals who gain even greater income from monetizing their brand. Some people make money by creating branded products and services in their names (i.e., Pat McGrath Labs®, Kylie Cosmetics®, Air Jordan®). With the growth of online buying power, even social media influencers are highly paid celebrities that make big bucks through brand collaborations. As a person's internet following increases on social media, they become more vulnerable to online infringement, so brand protection has become vital for everyday entrepreneurs who can go viral with one Facebook® post. In other words, personal branding and business branding can overlap, so when you are developing a protectable brand strategy, you must consider the success potential of everything connected to you and start with a strong brand foundation.

DO YOUR RESEARCH

As you create your business name, logos, slogans, or a combination thereof, you need to do your research. Your research level will not be the same as an attorney, but doing some basic research will prevent headaches later and save you some bucks. You need to use online search engines, your state business search features, social media, and even the USPTO website to determine if you are trying to launch a brand that is already in use. If that is the case, consult with an attorney before you move forward. If someone is using your brand, please consult with an attorney.

You can do a basic brand research right now. Yes, now! Record your findings below. If you need to consult with an attorney, commit to speaking to someone this week. Suppose you need to discuss a federal trademark application or a brand protection strategy. In that case, you can schedule an appointment with my office online at www.michellejmillerlaw.com or schedule time with another attorney that focuses on this area of law.

_____

_____

_____

After you have done your research, you need to determine your brand's strength, especially if you have a national target market. The stronger your brand, the more likely the USPTO will approve it for federal trademark registration. As you read this guide, the words "brand," "mark," and "trademark" will be used interchangeably depending on this topic.

A WEAK BRAND vs. A STRONG BRAND

As mentioned earlier in this chapter, creating a strong brand is crucial to the brand protection process. A strong brand is unique and easy to remember. A strong brand plays a vital role in how you market your products and services. A strong brand serves as a source identifier that may be eligible for federal protection as a registered trademark with the USPTO. A strong brand uniquely identifies your business, and it differentiates your business from other businesses in your industry. From a legal brand protection perspective, the stronger the brand, the more likely it qualifies for federal trademark registration. On the brand protection continuum, weak brands are generic and descriptive, which cannot be registered as a trademark. On the other hand, distinctive, arbitrary, and fanciful brands can be registered.

A Generic Brand

A generic brand is not a protectable brand. Generic brands are the weakest type of brands, and they are ineligible for trademark registration with the USPTO. A generic brand is one that applies to the good it represents. For example, "apple" would be considered a generic name for a fruit brand, but not for a laptop. Another example is the owner of the brand "Hotels.com" cannot trademark the word "hotel" because its website offers hotel reservations. Everyone has a right to use a generic term, so one person cannot claim that they should have the exclusive right to use the word as an exclusive brand.

As mentioned above, a popular generic brand name is brand is Hotels.com.

The owner of Hotels.com tried to obtain a federal trademark registration, but the USPTO denied the application. In denying the application, the USPTO concluded that the brand name was generic, and adding .com did not make the brand distinctive. Hotels.com engaged in a long and expensive legal battle over trademark registration. However, it simply cannot stop every other company in the lodging industry from using the word "hotel" because it is a generic term for that industry. Thus, Hotels.com is not a protectable brand.

A Descriptive Brand

A descriptive brand is exactly is a brand that describes a good or service. A descriptive brand describes the intended use, purpose, or function of a good or service. If the average person can easily correlate your brand name with its characteristics, it is a descriptive brand, and it is a usually weak brand. A descriptive brand may qualify for trademark registration if the owner demonstrates that the brand has achieved "secondary meaning" beyond the literal definition of the mark. Secondary meaning occurs when consumers associate the brand directly with the business rather than merely a general description of the company's primary commercial activity.

A descriptive brand can be registered as a trademark sometimes, enforcing it could be difficult because the brand is a standard description for a good or service. For example, cold is a description of ice cream. Crunchy is a description for potato chips. In general, I recommend that a client refrains from selecting a descriptive phrase as a brand name. Adopting a descriptive brand is a choice, and if used, it may require that you spend extra bucks policing your brand or eventually starting over with a new brand name. Protect your bucks and refrain from adopting a descriptive brand because the cost of trying to protect it, even if registered with the USPTO, might be too high. Obtaining a federal trademark registration for a descriptive brand is not impossible, but it is rare. A popular descriptive brand name is the brand Pizza Hut®[1].

---

[1] All product and company names used herein are trademarks™ or registered® trademarks of their respective holders. Use of them does not imply any affiliation with or endorsement by them.

A Suggestive Brand

A suggestive brand does not describe a product or service. However, there is a fine line between a descriptive brand and a suggestive brand. A suggestive brand name is related to a good or service, but it does not describe it. There is a thin line between a descriptive brand and a suggestive brand. A suggestive brand does not merely describe your goods or services; it makes you think about the brand related to your goods or services. In other words, a suggestive brand encourages the use of your imagination. If you create a suggestive brand name, it may qualify for registration with the USPTO. A popular brand name that is suggestive is the brand KitchenAid®[2]. The KitchenAid® brand makes a person think about what products can aid a person in a

---

[2] All product and company names used herein are trademarks™ or registered® trademarks of their respective holders. Use of them does not imply any affiliation with or endorsement by them.

kitchen without knowing its products. As such, the brand is not descriptive; it is suggestive and protectable.

KitchenAid®

An Arbitrary Brand

An arbitrary brand is a strong brand, and it is often protectable with USPTO registration. An arbitrary brand has a common name used in an uncommon manner. An arbitrary brand has no relation to your goods or services. If the brand is related to your goods or services, it is generic and not a protectable brand. For example, earlier in the chapter, I mentioned that apple is the common word for the fruit, while apple is not a generic brand for laptops. Apple®[3] is not a generic brand for laptops because the definition for the word apple is not related to laptops, computers, cell

---

[3] All product and company names used herein are trademarks™ or registered® trademarks of their respective holders. Use of them does not imply any affiliation with or endorsement by them.

phones, or even music. Apple® is an example of an arbitrary brand.

Apple

Fanciful (Coined) Brand

A fanciful brand is the strongest brand on the brand protection continuum. Fanciful brands are made-up names that do not have an actual dictionary definition. A fanciful brand did not exist until someone created it. Therefore, a fanciful brand is inherently unique and distinctive and is therefore entitled to the greatest legal protection. Choosing a fanciful brand gives you the exclusive right to its use. It is easy to prevent competitors from using a fanciful brand and profiting from it. An example of a famous fanciful brand is Adidas®[4]

---

[4] All product and company names used herein are trademarks™ or registered® trademarks of their respective holders. Use of them does not imply any affiliation with or endorsement by them.

Adidas® was founded by Adolf "Adi" Dassler, who began creating the sports shoes in his mother's laundry room. This fanciful brand is unique and distinctive; therefore, trademark law gives it the highest brand protection level.

How does your brand rank along the brand continuum? Identify ways you can improve the strength of your brand.

_____

_____

_____

_____

_____

_____

_____

BRAND PROTECTION CONTINUUM

 GENERIC = WEAKEST BRAND

 DESCRIPTIVE

 SUGGESTIVE

 ARBITRARY

 **FANCIFUL = STRONGEST BRAND**

3

TRADEMARKS 101

"Your brand is your trademark, and just like you are unique, your brand should be unique." – Michelle J. Miller-Boston

What exactly is a trademark? I am glad you asked. A trademark is simply your brand; it is how you identify your products and services. A trademark is a type of intellectual property that consists of a word, a phrase, a symbol, a design, or a combination of words, phrases, symbols, or designs that distinguishes the source of your goods and services from someone else. Intellectual property is intangible property. Real property (i.e., a home) is tangible property, and you can touch it. The most well-known intellectual property areas are patents, trademarks, copyrights, and trade secrets. Many people know that real property has value, but few people understand that intellectual property is valuable. However, let's take a moment to define the aforementioned intellectual property terms because people often mix up these terms' meanings.

INTELLECTUAL PROPERTY

Patents: Inventions, Processes or Compositions.

Example: Voice-Activated Car

Copyright: Original Literary, Artistic, Dramatic, and Musical Works.

Example: Movie Script

Trade Secrets: Compilation of Information, Designs, Practices, Patterns, or Formulas not known to the public.

Example: Customer Lists

Trademarks: Words, Logo, Slogans, or Images that are the source of goods or services.

Example: Clothing Line

An individual or company may need to register a patent, copyright, a trademark, and implement the appropriate protocols to protect its trade secrets. This book was designed as a guide to help you understand the importance of protecting your brand, business, and bucks with trademark registration.

A trademark and other creative property are intangible; you cannot touch them. Many people are taught to dumb down their creative genius, but that may be a mistake because one creative idea can lead to a million-dollar business venture. By protecting your brand through federal trademark registration, you protect the brand known as the source for your business bucks.

As mentioned in the last chapter, a strong brand (trademark) is vital to building a protectable brand. A strong brand is almost always protectable, and it usually receives full legal rights as an exclusive national brand after the USPTO approves your brand's registration. Federal trademark registration has significant benefits, but it is not a legal requirement.

TRADEMARK MYTHS

Before we go any further, I want to clear up some trademark myths. People often fail to protect their brands because of trademark myths. There have been countless times I've asked people do they have a registered trademark, and they enthusiastically answer "YES"!!! Being the person I am, I nod my head and then look it up only to find that the brand is not registered. Let's bust these trademark myths with some facts so you can handle your business.

Trademark Myth: Domain name ownership equals trademark ownership.

Trademark Fact: Fact is you do not own a trademark because you own a domain name. Also, owning a trademark does not automatically mean you own the domain name.

Trademark Myth: Owning a common law, an unregistered trademark, can prevent someone from obtaining a trademark registered with the USPTO.

Trademark Fact: Fact is you can assert your common law trademark right by using the ™

symbol. Your common law trademark rights may LIMIT the trademark rights of someone who registers a brand on a federal level, but it does not automatically prevent federal trademark registration.

Trademark Myth: Registration of a business name equals ownership of a trademark.

Trademark Fact: The fact is you do not have a trademark because you register a business name with the state. In addition, you cannot prevent other people from registering that business name in another state because you do not have a trademark registered with the USPTO.

Trademark Myth: You cannot trademark a color.

Trademark Fact: Under certain circumstances, you can trademark a color that is the source of your goods or services. Tiffany® signature blue color is a registered trademarked, the UPS® brown truck is registered, and even the famous red bottom shoes of Louboutin® is registered.[5]

Trademark Myth: You cannot trademark a scent.

Trademark Fact: Fact is, although unusual, you can register a trademark of a scent. I was recently reading about how the owner of Play-Doh obtained a trademark of its scent. I distinctly remember the smell of Play-Doh, and it truly is the source of that brand.

TRADEMARK RIGHTS

There are three levels of trademark rights within the United States. Those rights are common law rights, state rights, and federal rights. You may also seek international trademark rights by registering your trademark in different countries. Your market reach and target market goals will

---

[5] All product and company names used herein are trademarks™ or registered® trademarks of their respective holders. Use of them does not imply any affiliation with or endorsement by them.

help you determine the level of trademark rights perfect for you. If your target market is citywide only, and your focus is on traditional local media such as local radio and print advertising, you may not need to register your trademark.

Suppose your target market is statewide only, and your focus is on traditional local and statewide media such as television, radio, print advertising, and statewide media opportunities. In that case, you may need to register your trademark with your state. If your target market is nationwide, and your focus is on social media, you may need to register your brand with the federal government.

Suppose you are like most people in this online information age; you are engaged in business online. In that case, you should strongly consider registering your trademark with the USPTO if you service customers across state lines. Trademark protection helps consumers distinguish one company's product or service from another. Trademark protection through registration prevents consumer confusion in the marketplace. I like to say trademark registration stops people from using your brand to make money off similar business products and services like yours. When you fail to protect your brand, you fail to protect your business, and you fail to protect your bucks by leaving a door open for others to make money off your creative genius. Read the next section very carefully and consider what the best approach for you is. If you have questions or concerns, I recommend consulting with an attorney.

Common-Law Trademark Rights

Trademark rights arise automatically when a seller uses a mark connected with selling goods and services in commerce. To declare your ownership of a common-law trademark, you should add the superscript "T.M." to it. Common law trademark rights arise automatically, subject to specific requirements, which grants the trademark owner the right to exclude others from adopting and using the mark in the trademark owner's geographic area. I'm sure you are wondering why should I or anyone else register a trademark if we automatically have certain rights. Your thoughts are legitimate, and I want to help you with those thoughts.

Common law rights apply to a specific "geographic area" only. For example, if you sell a product in Chicago, IL, you may assert trademark rights within the Chicago city limits.

However, it's doubtful that you will be able to stop someone in Champaign, IL, from using the same trademark. Your trademark rights might not even extend to Evanston, IL, a township approximately 30 minutes north of Chicago. A common law trademark rights may preserve your rights in your geographic area even if someone registers the same trademark on a federal level. However, enforcing this right is extremely difficult because there is no official public record of your trademark. You risk your business's growth potential and your bucks when you rely only on a common law trademark.

State Trademark Rights

A state trademark registration provides trademark rights within the jurisdiction of the state where the application is filed. The rights afforded to trademark owners in one state may differ from those same rights in another state. A state trademark registration gives the trademark owner exclusive right to use the trademark in that state connected with the goods and services specified in the certificate, subject to any conditions and limitations stated in the certificate. To declare your ownership of a state law trademark, you should also add a superscript "T.M." to it. You usually register your trademark with the state office in most states, usually the Secretary of State. Once you register your brand with your state, there is an official record of your trademark and the first date of use. However, this does not cover you for the other states. Your state trademark rights may limit the rights of a person who seeks a federal registration of the same mark, but it does not prevent the federal registration. Imagine you having trademark ownership in one state and the trademark owner having trademark ownership in the other forty-nine states. For some people, that's not a bad deal. If you are not doing business in the other forty-nine states likelihood of confusion is a non-issue.

Federal Trademark Rights

Federal trademark rights are the highest level of trademark rights within the United States. A business in Chicago, IL, with a federal trademark registration, can use its rights to prevent someone from Chicago and anywhere in I.L. from using the trademark on similar goods and services. Also, the Chicago, IL business owner can stop someone in

California, Texas, New York, and anywhere else in the U.S.A. from using the trademark on similar goods and services. A federal trademark is national in scope regardless of your geographic use of your brand. As long as you are using your brand across state lines, you can obtain a federal trademark and prevent goods and services similar to yours from being sold in all fifty (50) states. After the USPTO registers your brand as a trademark, you get to declare your ownership of a federal trademark. After federal registration, you have the privilege of using the registered trademark symbol - ®. You engage in illegal conduct if you use the ® symbol with a brand you have not registered with the USPTO.

BENEFITS OF TRADEMARK REGISTRATION

There are several benefits to federal trademark registration. The benefits of setting aside a reasonable amount of money to protect your brand far outweighs the risk of doing nothing. You protect your business and bucks when you protect your brand. Immediately below are some of the possible benefits of having your trademark registered:

- official documentation and the legal presumption of national ownership of a trademark;
- right to use the ® symbol when you use your mark for the goods and services listed in the registration;
- the exclusive rights to operate and market the registered trademark on a national level;
- enlisting the power of the U.S. Government in helping to prevent trademark infringement at no additional cost to you;
- the ability to bring an action in federal court and walk into court with the presumption of trademark ownership validity;
- entitlement to treble damages (three times the proven damages) if there is a loss of business due to a violation of your trademark; and
- the protection against imports of similarly branded goods from offshore manufacturers under the protection of the U.S. Customs and Border Patrol Office.

What is your current level of trademark rights for each of your brand types? Do you need to change your level of brand protection to increase your trademark rights?

_____

_____

_____

There are many benefits to getting your brand registered with the USPTO. An unregistered brand is a brand at risk of infringement.

TRADEMARK INFRINGEMENT

Trademark infringement is the unauthorized use of a trademark on or in connection with goods or services in a manner that causes marketplace confusion. If a trademark owner believes trademark infringement has occurred, the first step is usually the issuance of a cease and desist letter. If the infringer does not stop using the trademark, the trademark owner may file a civil lawsuit in either state court or federal court for trademark infringement. Only trademark owners with a federal trademark registration can file a legal action in federal court. In court, the trademark owner (plaintiff) must prove that it owns a valid trademark and the alleged infringer's (defendant) use of the trademark causes marketplace confusion. If the USPTO registers your brand, there is a legal presumption of the mark's validity and ownership and the exclusive right to use the mark on a nationwide basis. If you're able to prove trademark infringement, the legal remedies available to you include the following:

- a court order (injunction) that the defendant stops using the accused mark;
- an order requiring the destruction or forfeiture of infringing items;
- monetary relief, including the defendant's profits, any damages sustained by the plaintiff, and the costs of the action, and

- an order that the defendant, in some instances, pays the plaintiffs' attorneys' fees.[6]

Now that we have been through these necessary initial steps, it is time to discuss the federal trademark application & registration process. In the next few chapters, I will present some essential information about protecting your brand (trademark) with the USPTO. Your brand(s) needs to be REGISTERED, and I hope that you can understand why trademark registration is vital at this point in the guide.

You are not legally required to obtain the services of an attorney to file a federal trademark application. However, filing a federal trademark application starts a legal proceeding, so if issues arise during the process, an understanding of trademark law's technical legal requirements is necessary. I often have people contact me who started the federal proceedings for a trademark application on their own or by using an online filing tool that cannot provide legal advice. I am often contacted because legal issues are presented during the proceedings, and people do not know how to respond because they lack legal

---

[6] USPTO website, "About Trademark Infringement", https://www.uspto.gov/page/about-trademark-infringement

knowledge. Many times people lose their money and have to start the process over with an attorney. Protect your bucks and hire a legal professional to help you with the trademark protection process.

4

TRADEMARK APPLICATION OVERVIEW

"The process may be long, and it may require work, but it's worth every minute."
– Michelle J. Miller-Boston

You created a strong, unique brand; now, it is time to protect it. Let's digger deeper into branding and how to execute a strategic brand band. Your brand band conveys different sounds, but they make beautiful music together. A strong, unique brand has the power to maximize all marketing opportunities from traditional media to social media at a quick pace on a local, state, national, or even international level. After identifying your brand, we will discuss the types of trademark applications needed to protect your brand band.

YOUR BRAND BAND

I recall playing the clarinet in my grade school band. Everyone who played an instrument in the band learned to play the same song, and we would sound great together (at least in my mind). There were times when each of us in the band would learn parts of a song while at other times, we all had to learn how to play an entire song with our instruments. When our band all learned the same song in its entirety, if I played the clarinet, someone would recognize the song, and if someone else played the saxophone, people would still recognize the same song. Your brand band should work just like this; different sounds but the same song. Here are the possible members of your brand band:

- ❖ Word(s)
- ❖ Logo
- ❖ Slogan
- ❖ Combination of Words with a Logo

As you assemble your brand band, remember that they make an incredible sound together. However, if one member of the brand band had to show up, people would recognize the brand. Every part of your brand band should point to your goods and services, and if only one member of your brand band plays an instrument, people should still recognize your goods and services. For example, Nike®[7] has an excellent brand band.

Nike, the Nike swoosh logo, and the Nike slogan, "just do it," make a beautiful brand melody together. If you use the Nike brand band together, you know that all point to the same products, and guess what? If you use any Nike brand band member alone, you will still think of the same products. If you see the famous swoosh, you are not thinking about another athletic apparel company; you instantly think about Nike even if you don't see the word "Nike." A strong brand band works together like our Nike example. Each member of the brand must be unique and strong for trademark registration success.

---

[7] All product and company names used herein are trademarks™ or registered® trademarks of their respective holders. Use of them does not imply any affiliation with or endorsement by them.

List your brand band below and decide in one or all members will be registered as a trademark:

_____

_____

_____

_____

REQUIREMENTS FOR A
TRADEMARK APPLICATION

You are now ready to get registered. You are ready to protect the brand! To get registered, you must be prepared to answer questions about your brand and your goods and services. You are not required to have a lawyer to complete the application for you. However, as mentioned earlier in this book, the trademark application process starts a legal proceeding, so I highly recommend that you hire a trademark attorney to prosecute your trademark application. There are three filing options for a United States trademark application. The three filing options are as follows:

o Intent to Use the Brand;

o Actual Use of the Brand; and

o Foreign application for a U.S.A. trademark.

Intent to Use Application

If you want to start the brand protection process before you launch, this is the application for you. This type of trademark application lets you reserve your trademark in the USPTO system before you start selling your products or offering your services. This trademark application option has an additional fee, but you also get time to complete your launch's final stages with your brand protection plan in the process. You also have the peace of knowing that you're not risking someone else beating you to the trademark line by applying the same brand name with the USPTO first. As an attorney who helps people protect their brands, I have several stories about people who procrastinate on starting the trademark application process. As a result, someone else beat them to the punch. If you get in line first, your prior pending trademark application prevents a later-filed application (of a confusingly similar brand) from proceeding in the trademark registration before the USPTO completes its review of your application. First in time is first in line with the USPTO.

Note: If you want to keep your upcoming launch a secret, this is not the application for you because trademark filings are public record. If you're going to launch and then file a trademark application at the earliest opportunity, you should discuss a strategy with your attorney.

Actual Use Application

If you are currently using your brand or your brand band in the marketplace, then the actual use application is the best application for you. To take advantage of this trademark application option, you must prove that you are using the brand in interstate commerce. A "specimen" is proof that you are using the brand in interstate commerce. Sometimes, I tell potential clients and clients it is "evidence" to help them understand what is required. I mean, a specimen does sound like its part of a science experiment. For this application, you need proof to demonstrate that you are selling a product and offering a service, and a photo of branded t-shirts in the trunk of your car will not work. The USPTO will register your brand as a trademark as long as your brand is strong, refer back to Chapter 2, and there are no prior registrations that will block yours.

Foreign Application

If you hold a U.S.A. trademark application and want to expand your brand globally, filing an international trademark is your next step. There is no such thing as a universal international trademark registration that protects your brand in every country. After the USPTO approves your U.S.A. trademark application and registers your trademark, you can use your U.S.A. application as a basis for filing a foreign application. If you have a foreign target market, you need to register your trademark n that country (or countries) is important.

If you have a pending trademark application in a foreign country, you can base your U.S.A. trademark application on it. A foreign applicant need not prove the use of its brand within the U.S.A. to register a trademark; the foreign applicant can rely solely upon the registration in his or her home country. A foreign applicant can base its U.S.A. trademark application date on its foreign trademark applicant's date. What does this mean? You can lose your trademark application priority to a foreign applicant. This loss of priority may occur even if your lawyer filed your trademark application with the USPTO first because the foreign applicant's home country registration date proceeds your U.S.A. trademark application date. In 2019, the USPTO released a rule that requires foreign applicants to have a U.S.A. attorney. If you are a foreign trademark applicant, you must hire an attorney licensed in the U.S.A. It is wise to hire an attorney with credentials like mine, an attorney who has trademark filing experience, and international business law experience.

The foreign trademark application option is based on international trademark treaties; I recommend that you consult an attorney about developing a global brand protection strategy.

What is the best trademark application for you?

_____

_____

5

THE TRADEMARK REGISTRATION PROCESS

"Your brand is valuable, so go through the process to protect your brand, your business, and your bucks." – Michelle J. Miller-Boston

L et's get started. You have gotten this far in the guide, and now it's time to go through the process for filing your trademark application to protect your brand, or shall I say your brand band. Good planning is vital to the trademark registration process to anticipate and create a response strategy for potential issues. The reality is that over fifty percent of all U.S.A. trademark applications receive an objection or rejection to registration, so do not fret. Good planning and a response strategy to potential issues will position your brand or brand band to proceed in the trademark registration process.

TRADEMARK OWNERSHIP

The first issue in the trademark registration process is what individual or entity will own the trademark. You may list one or more individuals as the trademark owner. You may also name a legal entity (i.e., L.L.C., Corporation, etc.) as the trademark owner. The trademark owner must exist before the application filing. You should not apply for a trademark and list a non-existent business because this would create a problem in the trademark registration process. If you have questions about trademark ownership, you should consult with an attorney. You will also have to list contact information for the owner(s) in the application, so be prepared to share an address, phone number, and email, all of which will become part of public records.

DEPICTION OF THE MARK

You need to identify the mark (brand) that you would like to protect. There are two options. Option 1 is a "wordmark," which is standard characters that protect the words. A wordmark is not limited to using specific font size, style, or size. The wordmark is typed into the required section in the application. Option 2 is a "design mark," which is a mark that includes the unique stylization of font and designs. If you have words combined with a design, you will use this second option. Your attorney must submit the design mark as a .jpg image. Although .png images our popular, this format is not acceptable in the USPTO system. You must have a .jpg version of the image. If the mark is uploaded in a specific color, that applicant can only use the specific color filed.

Immediately below are examples of each type of mark.

Example Word Mark:

The M. J. MILLER Law Firm®

Example Design Mark:

THE
M.J.MILLER
——LAW FIRM——

TRADEMARK CLASSES

Your trademark application covers your brand's exclusive use within a specific trademark class or classes listed within the USPTO's list of categories. You must be using your brand or have a bona fide intent to use your brand in connection with a specific class of goods or services. Goods are products. Services are activities. The USPTO identification manual identifies forty-five classes. The Trademark Manual of Examining Procedures (T.M.E.P.) 1401.02(a) breaks the classes into two categories: goods and services. The first thirty-four classes cover goods while the last ten classes cover services. The forty-five classes listed in TMEP 1401.02(a) are as follows:

GOODS

Class 1	Chemicals
Class 2	Paints
Class 3	Cosmetics & cleaning preparations
Class 4	Lubricants & fuels
Class 5	Pharmaceuticals
Class 6	Metal goods
Class 7	Machinery
Class 8	Hand tools
Class 9	Electrical & scientific apparatus
Class 10	Medical apparatus
Class 11	Environmental control apparatus
Class 12	Vehicles
Class 13	Firearms
Class 14	Jewelry
Class 15	Musical instruments
Class 16	Paper goods and printed matter
Class 17	Rubber goods
Class 18	Leather goods

Class 19	Nonmetallic building materials
Class 20	Furniture & articles not otherwise classified
Class 21	Housewares & glass
Class 22	Cordage and fibers
Class 23	Yarn and threads
Class 24	Fabrics
Class 25	Clothing
Class 26	Fancy goods
Class 27	Floor covering
Class 28	Toys and sporting goods
Class 29	Meats & processed foods
Class 30	Staple foods
Class 31	Natural agricultural products
Class 32	Light beverages
Class 33	Wines & spirits
Class 34	Smoker's articles

SERVICES

Class 35	Advertising and business
Class 36	Insurance & financial
Class 37	Building construction & repair
Class 38	Telecommunications
Class 39	Transportation & storage

Class 40   Treatment of materials

Class 41   Education & entertainment

Class 42   Computer and scientific

Class 43   Hotels & restaurants

Class 44   Medical, beauty & agricultural

Class 45   Personal and legal

Your identification of goods and services cannot be one of the class headings listed above. Identifying goods and services must fit within one of the classes, and the class must be correct. The language used to describe goods or services should be understandable to the average person and should not require an in-depth knowledge of the relevant field. An applicant can use the language directly from the manual and or draft a specific language for review.

The accuracy of the original application's identification language is important because the identification cannot be expanded later.[8] Thus, once your trademark application is filed, you cannot add more classes to your application. Your attorney may request the removal of goods and services, but

---

[8] *See* 37 C.F.R. §2.71(a); TMEP §§1402.06 et seq. and 1402.07 et seq.; In re M.V Et Associes, 21 USPQ2d 1628 (Comm'r Pats. 1991).

61

your attorney cannot add more goods and services. Goods and services can be made more specific or clarified in the application process, but your attorney cannot broaden them. For example, you have a t-shirt brand; you cannot later change it to t-shirt design services. After your attorney identifies the goods and services, he or she will calculate your USPTO application fees.

FILING FEES

The USPTO application fees are nonrefundable. Your USPTO filing fees are based on the number of classes listed within your trademark application and the type of application filed. Each trademark application type has specific filing requirements, so discussing the best application type with an attorney is recommended. The trademark application types are as follows:

- TEAS Plus
- TEAS Regular
- Paper – *only under limited circumstances as of February 15, 2020*

The TEAS Plus application and all communications relating to it are done electronically, and this application has the lowest USPTO application fee. The TEAS Regular application is also filed online and is the next level of fees. The Paper application has the highest fee; it is not done online. Typically, an attorney will charge you their legal fee, plus the USPTO fee, as well as a retainer that will go into a trust account. If you complete your application without an attorney's assistance, the USPTO will likely recommend that you seek the help of an attorney in the process because legal knowledge is needed to address all legal issues.

USPTO ATTORNEY REVIEW

The USPTO assigns an attorney to review each application for review (Examining Attorney). The USPTO usually assign an Examining Attorney to a trademark application within three months of the initial filing date. The Examining Attorney will review the application for compliance with technical filing and legal requirements.

If your application does not meet all the technical filing and legal requirements, there will be an objection to your application, or your trademark registration will be rejected. As mentioned earlier, a large number of applications receive disapproval or rejection. However, this is not the end of the application process. The Examining Attorney will issue an Office Action, which will identify all issues with the application. Upon receipt of the Office Action, an answer must be filed within six months, or the USPTO considers the application abandoned. If your attorney cannot fix the errors in the application, you must restart the application process.

List your questions or concerns about your trademark application that you want to discuss with an attorney before filing. You may need to schedule a legal consultation to receive answers and guidance.

_____

_____

_____

_____

COMMON OBJECTIONS & REJECTION ISSUES

Immediately below is a non-exhaustive list of issues that may arise during the trademark proceedings. Immediately below are issues that generally occur during the Examining Attorney's review of a trademark application.

OBJECTIONS

Proof of Use Does Not Match Trademark

Your specimen (or evidence) demonstrates your proof of trademark use. If your specimen does not match the wordmark or the design mark filed, the Examining Attorney will object to its use. To overcome this objection, the applicant must resubmit a new specimen with a signed declaration or convert the application type.

Classes and Fees Paid Do Not Match

You must pay a fee for each trademark class listed within your trademark application. If you or your attorney file an application and the fee submitted is incorrect, the Examining Attorney will object to your application moving to the next stage in the proceeding. You will need to pay the appropriate fees for your application to move forward in the proceeding.

Unclear Identification of Goods & Services

Your attorney must identify the goods and services accurately in your application. What does this mean? You must have well-defined goods and services before filing your trademark application. If your goods and services are unclear, the Examining Attorney will identify an objection to your application. Your attorney must clarify your goods and services for the application to proceed in the process.

Unclear Color Claim

Your trademark application must depict if you are claiming a brand color or not. If you submit a specimen that contains colors, but your application states that you are not claiming colors, there will be an objection to your application. To the same end, if you claim color and a color description is unclear or inaccurate, there will be an objection to your application. A clarification of your color claim will be needed for your application to proceed.

REJECTIONS

Merely Descriptive

If your brand describes your goods or services, your trademark application will be rejected. The purpose of having a strong brand is to ensure that it distinguishes your goods and services from others in the marketplace, and a mere description does not accomplish this. Your brand must be distinctive, not descriptive. If your brand conveys knowledge about or a function of your goods or services, it is descriptive. If your brand represents a characteristic of your goods or services, it is descriptive. If you are selling mango candles, which I love, the word MANGO in your brand is descriptive of the candle. Descriptive words are available for public use, and the USPTO will not register it as a trademark without a lengthy and often long and expensive strategic brand development plan.

Failure to Prove Trademark Use

Proof of your brand's actual use in commerce is an absolute necessity to obtain a trademark registration. There are numerous technical and legal requirements regarding the use of a brand in commerce. If your proof of use does not meet the appropriate requirements, the USPTO will reject your application. It is important for your marketing, advertising, and promotional material to present your brand correctly to the public. Your brand should be presented in a clear, consistent manner in connection with your goods and services. Your brand must appear consistently to ensure that you have options. Display your brand, as listed in the application, on your product packaging, your P.O.S. (point-of-sale) display, and of course, the actual product itself. The Examining Attorney will review your website, so it is crucial to have your brand displayed in a prominent location, along with your products or services, along with a way to make a purchase.

Confusingly Similar

If your brand is confusingly similar to an already registered brand, your trademark application will be rejected. Your brands do not have to be identical; they only need to be confusingly similar. Actual confusion between your mark and another mark is not required; there only has to be a likelihood of confusion. The following will not overcome a likelihood of confusion rejection:

- Changing the spelling
- Making the mark possessive
- Making the mark plural
- Adding punctuation marks

If someone has a pending application that is likely to be confusingly similar to your brand, it may slow down the registration process. In that case, the USPTO will suspend your application until it makes a decision about the prior-filed application. The Examining Attorney will also review the goods and services to determine if they are related. The goods and services do not have to be identical; the USPTO may reject your trademark because it is too related to a registered trademark. The Examining Attorney will allow an attorney to overcome this rejection, but from my experience, this rejection is difficult to overcome. If the brand is similar, but the goods and services are not related to your application, your application will move to the next stage in the trademark proceeding.

Geographically Identifiers

If your brand's primary significance is a known geographic location, the USPTO may reject your application. If the goods or services originated in that geographic location and potential customers would likely believe your goods or services created in the geographic area identified in your brand, your trademark application will be rejected. Many local companies use the name of a township, city, or even the state as an identifier, but they cannot register most of them as a trademark.

Surnames

Often, a business owner creates their brand name on the last name or the brand owner's family name. The USPTO will usually register surname brands if they are rare are more likely to be distinctive. Surnames might be registerable under certain unique circumstances. You may also register a surname if your attorney can provide it's truly a brand.

In most of the instances described above, the Examining Attorney will issue an Office Action and provide an opportunity to overcome the objection or rejection within six months. If the USPTO refuses to register your brand on the Primary Register, it may be eligible for registration to the Supplemental Register. The general public cannot distinguish between whether your trademark is registered to the Primary Register or the Supplemental Register when they look at it.

OFFICE ACTIONS

The objections and rejections identified by the Examining Attorney may become the basis of an Office Action. In most cases, the Office Action will be non-final, and your attorney must file an answer within six months.

If applicable, use this section to identify any of your Trademark Office Action questions or concerns:

_____

_____

If the Office Action's answer is persuasive to the Examining Attorney, the application will move on to the next phase of the proceeding. If the answer is not compelling to the Examining Attorney, the application will not move on to the next step of the proceeding; the USPTO will issue a Final Office Action.

PUBLICATION

Publication in the Official Gazette is the next stage of the trademark application proceedings. If you overcome the objections and rejections of the Examining Attorney or if there are no objections or rejections to your trademark application, he or she will publish your trademark, and third parties will have thirty days to challenge its registration. Within these thirty days, any party can file an opposition to registration or an extension to file an opposition. If someone files an opposition, the USPTO assigns the opposition to the Trademark Trial and Appeal Board. If there are no oppositions, the trademark application will proceed to registration. If you filed an intent-to-use application and there are no oppositions to the trademark application, A Notice of Allowance will issue, and you will be given six months to demonstrate your use of the brand.

The entire trademark application proceedings can take at least one year. If Office Actions are issued, or extensions are requested, the application process may take almost two years or longer. The process is worth it for your peace of mind, so please be patient.

REGISTRATION

Cue the confetti and shouts of joy; a congratulation is in order! If you have been through this entire process, your brand is protected because you are now officially REGISTERED (or you know the basic steps necessary to get registered)! You have waited a year or longer, and now the day of celebration is finally here. You now have the legal right to use the ® symbol with your brand. You have the right to proclaim national brand exclusivity for the goods or services listed in your trademark application.

Guess what? You have more work to do; you must police and monitor your registered trademark. You must enforce your federal trademark rights!

6

AFTER REGISTRATION

—————⸙—————

"A registered trademark owner walks in power and authority, use it!"
– Matthew 24:30 (N.K.J.V.)

Use your federal trademark rights. You must police and monitor your registered trademark to maintain your registration. A trademark registration gives you brand power, but you also have brand responsibility. Your must utilize and maintain control over your brand. Yes, your brand is protected. However, to keep your marketplace exclusivity and power, you must police your trademark. You also need to note important maintenance and renewal filings necessary to retain your registered trademark status. This chapter will receive a few tips regarding steps you should take after the USPTO your trademark registers your trademark.

ENFORCE YOUR BRAND

You must enforce your federal trademark rights. If a third-party use your brand without your authorization or permission, you need to do something about it. Allowing third parties to use your trademark will weaken your trademark and could potentially make it generic in your industry. If you believe trademark infringement has occurred, gather evidence that shows the alleged infringement and have a consultation with your attorney. You have a right to stop people from using your trademark without your permission, and policing your brand will allow you to identify issues as soon as possible.

MAINTAIN CONTROL OF YOUR BRAND

Trademark infringement can happen almost anywhere, especially in the age of social media. When it comes to your registered trademark, you must exercise your brand muscle by flexing on brand perpetrators. Social media is an area where trademark infringement happens often, and if you do not exercise your rights, it can get out of control. You should own the social media usernames for your brand because this will help consumers identify your brand quickly and easily. If you identify trademark infringement on social media, you should follow the social media procedures to report infringing conduct. You should also maintain control of your brand reputation on social media sites.

POLICE YOUR BRAND

It would be best if you policed your trademark. Just scream (even if to yourself), STOP TRADEMARK THIEF! It is your responsibility to identify and stop improper and unauthorized use of your trademark. You should periodically use internet search engines, and you should also search social media sites to determine if people are improperly using your brand. If you identify any issues, consult with your attorney.

MONITOR YOUR BRAND

Monitoring your brand is akin to policing your brand. By monitoring your brand and its usage, you can effectively protect your brand and your business's value. You should establish or obtain a brand monitoring program to ensure people entering the marketplace are not trying to use a brand that is confusingly similar to your brand.

MANAGE YOUR BRAND USAGE

You must also take the necessary steps to maintain your trademark registration. Your attorney may offer monitoring services after the USPTO registers your trademark; this will ensure that your trademark registration isn't lost. It would be best to educate people on using your brand, even your affiliates such as licensees, distributors, and franchisees. Your must manage how other people utilize your brand.

DECLARATION OF CONTINUED USE

You must affirm that you are still selling the products or services covered by your trademark application. This affirmation is done by filing a Declaration of Continued Use between the 5th and 6th year following your trademark registration date. If you fail to file the Declaration of Continued Use, the USPTO will cancel your trademark registration. Please contact your attorney if you need help.

10-YEAR RENEWAL PERIODS

There is an ongoing responsibility to renew your trademark registration. Before the 10th year from the date of your trademark registration and then every ten years after that, you must file a trademark renewal. If you fail to file the renewal, the USPTO will cancel your trademark registration.

CONGRATULATIONS!

Taking the time to learn how to protect your brand, business, and bucks with trademark registrations is one of the most important things you could have done for yourself. Protecting your brand by obtaining federal (and even international) trademark registration is one of the best investments that you can make in your business, so kudos to you! Your brand may just become one of your most valuable business assets

7

MONETIZING YOUR TRADEMARK

———————— ❧ ————————

"Intellectual Property, like trademarks, is valuable intangible property, so treat your creative genius like the next billion-dollar idea."

– Michelle J. Miller-Boston

Monetize your trademark! Monetizing your registered trademarks can bring substantial new revenue streams to your business or businesses. Protecting your brand through trademark registration is not just an opportunity for you to preserve your brand from getting used by another person or company – it is also a way to make money. As of 2019, Amazon is the most valuable brand at $315.5 billion; Amazon is the second most valuable brand at $309.5 billion, and then Google is the third most valuable brand at $309 billion.[9] These brands did not start as multi-billion-dollar brands, but I'm sure the owners had the vision to grow a ridiculously valuable brand. I want you to think big and handle your vision according to your thoughts and not your current circumstances. This chapter contains some monetization tactics. You should not engage in any of these potential monetization tactics without consulting with your attorney.

LICENSING

Trademark licensing is very common. You grant someone the right to use your trademark for a fee. When you grant a license to use your brand, you provide the licensee with the authority to make and distribute specific products or services according to a trademark licensing agreement. As the licensor, you will receive a certain amount of money or royalties in exchange for sharing your registered trademark. Licensing is a great way to monetize your brand.

---

[9] https://www.cnbc.com/2019/06/11/amazon-beats-apple-and-google-to-become-the-worlds-most-valuable-brand.html

ONLINE SALES

You may have the potential to make passive income with your branded products or services. If you are selling branded t-shirts out of a retail store, you can increase your sales by offering your products online. By offering your products online, you can make money 24-hours a day. Because you have a registered trademark that you are monitoring, you are not concerned about other people making money due to your brand's unauthorized use. You are in control of your business, and you are in control of your brand. Because your brand is protected, you have marketplace exclusivity for your goods and services, so you work smarter and not harder.

CO-BRANDING

Co-branding allows both trademark owners to take advantage of each other's strengths and trademarks. In a co-branding situation, the parties generally create a new co-branded product that both parties make money. Co-branding has become quite popular, especially in the food industry and make-up industry. When you have a registered trademark, your brand is official, and it is protected, so registered trademark owners will not see working with you as a risk to their brand asset. Co-branding is an excellent way to attract more consumers and enhance your sales. Co-branding is a great way to monetize your brand.

OBTAINING FINANCING

Did you know you can use the value of intellectual property to generate financing? Well, yes, you can. Just like any other valuable asset, trademarks can be used as security to obtain capital if they are valuable. A registered trademark owner may use a trademark as collateral commonly secured in a "security interest" agreement.[10] Using your brand to obtain funds is one of the most challenging ways to use registered trademarks to get money. However, one study showed that using a trademark as collateral, through a trademark assignment, increased from 2002 through 2015 even though the percentage is small.[11] Monetizing your brand to obtain financing is a viable option, but this requires careful consideration and strategic planning.

Take steps to build a strong and influential brand, and the money-making opportunities will be endless. Once you have protected your brand, you may rest in the fact that money cometh to wise business owners with a powerful brand vision. Remember, you can also assign your trademark, leave your trademark ownership to someone in a will, or you can even sell your trademark. The options of what you can do as a registered trademark owner are almost endless.

---

[10] Monetizing the Marks: Insight from the USPTO Trademark Assignment Database, https://onlinelibrary.wiley.com/doi/full/10.1111/jems.12261

[11] The Puzzle in Financing Trademark Collateral, https://houstonlawreview.org/article/6778-the-puzzle-in-financing-with-trademark-collateral

8

CONCLUSION

It's time for your brand to shine in the marketplace. You've made a wise investment in this book. Hopefully, you have planned or will plan to invest in obtaining the legal services of an attorney that can help you develop a plan to protect your brand, business, and bucks with trademarks. With the internet, we live in a world without borders, and your brand can go viral with one mouse click. If you have a brand and have not started the trademark registration process – now is the time to start. I want to wrap up this guide by giving you some additional words of wisdom and a few warnings.

WORDS OF WISDOM & WARNINGS

You have three options for filing a federal trademark application. Those three options are (1.) file yourself, (2) use a discount filing service, or (3.) hire an experienced attorney. Filing a trademark application may seem deceptively simple, but there are many technical and legal requirements.

Regarding option 1, you risk your business and your bucks if you start a legal proceeding that you do not know how to handle. Remember, the USPTO does not issue refunds, and many times people who file their own applications have to start the process over using a lawyer.

Regarding option 2, unbeknownst to most people, it is almost the same as option 1. When you use a discount-rate trademark filing service like *Trademarkia, Trademark Plus, Trademark Engine, or LegalZoom*, you are merely using a do-it-yourself platform that offers no legal feedback. These discount-rated-services generally have forms for you to fill out online. The non-lawyers who may answer questions cannot give your legal advice because that would be considered the unauthorized practice of law.

The best option, option 3, is to obtain a lawyer's services that understand the trademark registration process. Don't gamble your brand, business, and bucks by taking an unnecessary risk with this federal process. When seeking an attorney, find one to make a part of your team and that you are willing to consider a trusted advisor.

FINAL WORDS

You are a million steps ahead of individuals that are still advertising and marketing an unprotected brand. Every week I speak to someone who tells me a story about how someone is using their brand. Wealthy people develop strategies that lead to success. Developing a strategy to protect your plan shows that you have the mindset like multi-billion-dollar business owners mentioned in this book.

I hope this will be a book that you pick up repeatedly as you protect your brand band. I wish you much success in all your endeavors. Maximize the use of your trademark and monetize it!

NOTES

Michelle J. Miller

ABOUT THE AUTHOR

Known as a passionate and encouraging lawyer, Michelle is a trusted advisor and legal counsel to entrepreneurs, entertainers, celebrities, influencers, coaches, authors, publishers, and world-renowned ministry leaders. Michelle J. Miller is the owner of The M. J. MILLER Law Firm®, a boutique law firm focused on helping visionaries build, protect, and grow their business from the neighbor to the nations. She is also the founder of The Law Box™. After simultaneously being lead regional counsel, lead worldwide operations counsel, and lead e-commerce counsel for a large corporation, Michelle took a leap of faith and started her legal practice. Michelle obtained her undergraduate degree from the University of Illinois at Urbana Champaign, her law degree from DePaul University College of Law, and her advanced law degree (L.L.M.) in International Business & Trade Law from the John Marshall Law School. Michelle has been to South Africa, Russia, Dubai, China & Singapore to learn and speak about legal issues. Michelle J. Miller resides in the Chicagoland area with her daughter, Heaven Miller. Michelle is available to speak, coach, and train on the content in this book.

CONTACT MICHELLE TODAY!

www.michellejmillerlaw.com

mjm@michellejmillerlaw.com

@michellejmilleresq

(312) 985-5200

www.ingramcontent.com/pod-product-compliance
Lightning Source LLC
Chambersburg PA
CBHW071515200326
41519CB00019B/5955